BOYD & EVANS

20 SEPTEMBER - 13 OCTOBER 1991

Flowers East

Raindog 1991
Oil on canvas
91.5 x 71 cms

Boyd & Evans' project as collaborative artists has been remarkably consistent in terms of its essential outlines, even if its development has involved some fascinating and significant shifts of emphasis. Their most recent work confirms this consistency, while revealing an increased sureness in both exploration and realisation.

They have worked for many years with the basic idea of investing an image of photographic (or quasi-photographic) illusionism with qualities that serve to open up a symbolic dimension. Luminosity, a sense of stillness (sometimes in relation to moving figures), visual shifts and discontinuities of various sorts, juxtapositions of disparate elements, as well as certain iconographic details – all these things, and more, would be relevant to a discussion of the relation of their 'high realist' techniques and conventions to questions of meaning and vision. What always 'holds' the observer, with a Boyd & Evans painting, is the primacy and efficacy of the visual image; but at the same time one is always aware that more is at stake than autonomous aesthetic criteria.

Their art is, first of all, an art of verisimilitude – of interpretation and possibility, or of 'hypothetical situations', to use their own terminology. There is, secondly, something like a parabolic intention in certain of their works; this is pursued in an utterly unpretentious, and sometimes humorous, way. Thirdly, there is a preoccupation (and it has become paramount in many paintings of more recent years) with disclosing an epiphanic moment of experience. By epiphany, I mean an apprehension of some invisible or suprasensible dimension, through attention to the particulars of the visible world. Boyd & Evans are concerned with what the Canadian realist painter Jack Chambers once referred to as 'that faculty of inner vision where the object appears in the splendour of its essential namelessness'. It is difficult to account for the precise way in which the paintings reveal this subtle and ineluctable splendour; for this seems so 'matter-of-fact', and so little tied to conventional notions of beauty. They provoke an intensification of our perception through very subtle 'breaks' – disparities, contrasts, irregularities – in a pictorial field that would otherwise show the mundane world as a thoroughly consistent reality. This serves to heighten the sense of stillness in such a way that it carries the epiphanic 'emission' which the paintings also thematize. Paintings from the later 1980s often deal with a figure (or figures) in a natural landscape, caught in (what appears to be) a state of absorption. Indeed, they seem to be enfolded by the reality they witness; in this respect, they bring to mind the figure/landscape (or seascape) relationship in certain of Caspar David Friedrich's paintings. The details of the paintings are observed with a calm yet heightened attention, so that these figures often seem mediators for the artists' vision, as much as the 'objects' of that vision. ('Witness', which Boyd & Evans used as the title of one of the screenprints in their serial work *Bird* (1990), seems most apt as a designation for such figures, absorbed in their seeing.)

Hidden Agenda 1990
Acrylic on canvas
152 x 152 cms

A related, but distinct tendency, has become very evident in the paintings of the past three years. Many of these most recent paintings explore the dialogic relations between inward and outward vision, and invisibility and visibility – which are paired rather than merely contrasted, and put into action in the permutative conjunctions of persons with other persons and with landscapes. The absorption that typifies epiphanic vision is thematized within a variety of 'hypothetical situations'. For example, in *Hidden Agenda* (1990), we are presented with a male figure in full light, and a woman, to the immediate right but some distance back from him, in shadow. The man gazes intently outwards, while the woman is inwardly absorbed. Both figures have their backs to a window through which we can see a landscape with a lake; the man holds a postcard of a painting in both hands, but isn't looking at it. (Boyd & Evans have used their own likenesses for the two figures, I might add.) The painting coheres through the tensions and connections it sustains between the various elements: outward gaze and inward absorption; the 'objects' of each, which remain invisible to us; the partially visible image of the postcard; the visible landscape (visible, that is, to us – but not to the figures); and, of course, the light and shadow, alternatively revealing or obscuring. Like Boyd & Evans' other work, it involves us in the tensions and complexities of its 'hypothetical situation', but without it being possible to simply resolve them in an act of rational comprehension. At the same time, the image involves us through its coherence and grace.

Other works that directly participate in these same concerns include *The Interpreter* (1990), *The Second Interpreter (*1990), *Looking Up* (1991), and *Passing By* (1991); while similar questions of inward and outward vision inform such paintings as *Sharing a Dream* (1989) and *The Man and the Island* (1989).

Untitled 1990
Acrylic on canvas
25.5 x 35 cms

By contrast, a painting like *Master of Activities* (1990) appears to hark back to the oneiric mood of certain earlier works – I am thinking particularly of *The Return* (1986) and *The Step's Tale* (1986). All of their work represents a search for ways of rupturing and opening up the mundane, and if certain themes and aspects are predominant at a given time, there are also interesting divergences from these predominant tendencies. What is most instructive about *Master of Activities*, perhaps, is the increase in subtlety since a work like *The Step's Tale*; indeed, *Master of Activities* is a remarkable feat in its combination of simplicity and mystery. The objects in the foreground, with their emphatic and solid yet hallucinatory presence, seem to open up a path running toward the man who stands beckoning by the tree in the middle distance, while at the same time forming an obstacle by their very ineluctability. The composition conjures a relationship between these objects (box and table), the man and the tree, and the blue wall at the left side of the picture – but one which remains, in terms of the image itself, elusive; despite any anecdotal "explanations" that may spring to mind.

Boyd & Evans' is an art that penetrates and uncovers, in a very undramatic but extremely moving and intelligent way. The paintings reveal their makers' engagement with human existence and with nature, and their probing of the complexities and problematics of vision – as much as their unstinting devotion to the demands of painting.

DAVID MILLER 1991

Second Interpreter 1990
Acrylic on canvas
152 x 152 cms

The Man and the Island 1990
Acrylic on canvas
91 x 121.5 cms

Straw Dog 1991
Oil on canvas
252 x 144 cms

The Small Divide 1991
Oil on canvas
61 x 91.5 cms

Looking Up 1991
Oil on canvas
61 x 91.5 cms

Against the Day 1991
Oil on canvas
122 x 122 cms

Guardians 1991
Oil on canvas
61 x 91.5 cms

Swan Song 1990
Acrylic on canvas
70.5 x 91.5 cms

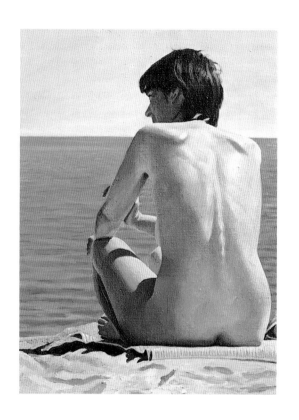

Untitled 1989
Acrylic on canvas
35 x 25.5 cms

The Interpreter 1990
Acrylic on canvas
91 x 90.5 cms

The Other Way 1990
Oil on canvas
84 x 115 cms

Guardians 1991
Oil on canvas
244 x 152.5 cms

Passing By 1991
Oil on canvas
76 x 274 cms

Focus 1989
Acrylic on canvas
122 x 122 cms

On the Wall 1990
Acrylic on canvas
90.5 x 137 cms

Master of Activities 1990
Acrylic on canvas
121.5 x 183 cms

Full Circle 1990
Acrylic on canvas
91 x 122 cms

BOYD & EVANS

1944	Boyd born
	Studied at Leeds University
1945	Evans born
	Studied at Leeds College of Art
1968	Started working together
1977/78	Spent a year travelling throughout America as Bi-Centennial Fellows

ONE PERSON EXHIBITIONS

1972/74/77/79	Angela Flowers Gallery, London
1972	Park Square Gallery, Leeds
1976	Boyd and Evans 1970-75, Turnpike Gallery, Leigh, Lancs
	Sheffield City Art Galleries
	Third Eye Centre, Glasgow
	Wolverhampton City Art Gallery
	Gainsborough's House, Sudbury
1978	Fendrick Gallery, Washington DC
	Graves Art Gallery, Sheffield
	Leicester City Museum
	Wolverhampton City Art Gallery
1980/82/84/86/88	Angela Flowers Gallery, London
1980	Spectro Arts Workshop, Newcastle
	Impressions Gallery, York
	Phoenix Gallery, Leicester
	Basel Art Fair, Switzerland
1981	Ton Peek, Utrecht
1982/83	A Decade of Paintings, Milton Keynes Exhibition Gallery
	Bede Gallery, Jarrow
	City Museum & Art Gallery, Stoke on Trent
	Ferens Art Gallery, Hull
1985	Milton Keynes Touring Exhibition
	Milton Keynes Exhibition Gallery
	Drumcroon Art Centre, Wigan
1990	Bird, Flowers East, London
	English Paintings, Brendan Walter Gallery, Santa Monica, USA
	Angela Flowers (Ireland) Inc. Rosscarbery, Ireland
1991	Flowers East, London

SELECTED GROUP EXHIBITIONS

1970	Narrative Painting in Britain in the 20th Century, Camden Arts Centre
	Postcards, Angela Flowers Gallery, London
1972	British Drawing 1952-1972, Angela Flowers Gallery, London
	Bradford Print Biennale (Prize)
1973	Imagini Come Strumenta di Realta, Studio la Citta, Verona
1974	Graveurs Anglais Contemporains, Cabinet des Estamps, Geneva
	6th Festival International de la Peinture, Cagnes-Sur-Mer, (First prize)
	Bradford Print Biennale
	John Moores Liverpool Exhibition
1974	New Image Painting, 1st Tokyo International Biennale of Figurative Art
1975	Delhi Triennale
	Body and Soul, Peter Moores, Liverpool
1976	British Realist Show, Ikon Gallery
	The Deck of Cards, JPL Fine Arts
1976/78	Aspects of Realism, Rothmans of Pall Mall, Canada
1978	10th Festival International de la Peinture, Cagne-Sur-Mer and Musee d'Art Moderne, Paris
1978/79	Certain Traditions, Recent British and Canadian Art, Touring Canada
1981	The Real British, Fischer Fine Art, London
1985	Black and White, Angela Flowers Gallery, London
	Attitudes, Northampton Central Museum
	Small is Beautiful Part 4, Angela Flowers Gallery, London
1986	Sixteen, Angela Flowers Gallery, London
1987	State of the Nation, Herbert Gallery, Coventry
1988	Contemporary Portraits, Flowers East, London
1989	Big Paintings, Flowers East, London
	The Thatcher Years, Flowers East, London
1989/90	Angela Flowers Gallery 1970/90, Barbican Concourse Gallery, London
1990	Small is Beautiful Part 8: The Figure, Flowers East, London
1991	Angela Flowers Gallery 1991, Flowers East, London

PUBLIC COLLECTIONS

Arts Council of Great Britain
British Council
Museum of Modern Art, New York
Sheffield City Art Gallery
Wolverhampton City Art Gallery
Leeds City Art Gallery
Contemporary Art Society
Leicester Education Authority
Tate Gallery
Bankers Trust
Readers Digest
West Wales Association for the Arts
Manchester City Art Gallery
Wigan Department of Leisure
Cabinet des Estamps, Geneva
Milton Keynes Development Corporation
Unilever Plc
Belfast Museum
Williamson Art Gallery
University College of Wales, Aberystwyth

BIBLIOGRAPHY

Bernard Denvir, Art International, February 1971

William Packer, Art and Artists, February 1971

Peter Fuller, Arts Review, July 1972

Jane Stockwood, Harpers and Queen, January 1972

Marina Vaizey, Financial Times, 4 July 1972

Eddie Wolfram, Art and Artists, July 1972

Peter Sagar, Neue Formen des Realismus. Kunst zwischen
Illusion und Wirklichkeit, 1973

Marina Vaizey, Imagini come Strumenta di Realta, catalogue
Studio la Citta Galleria D'arte Verona, 1973

Richard Smart, Arts Review, July 1974

Marina Vaizey, Sunday Times, July 1974

Leigh Merete Bates, The Guardian, 13 April 1975

William Feaver, The Observer Review, 27 February 1977

Edward Lucie-Smith, Illustrated London News, February 1977

Michael Shepherd, Sunday Telegraph, 27 February 1977

Paul Overy, The Times, 1 March 1977

Artefact, May 1979

Observer Magazine, 1 April 1979

Mel Gooding, Arts Review, 7 November 1980

Fenella Crichton, Boyd and Evans: Drawings Catalogue
Angela Flowers Gallery, 1982

Robert Heller, Boyd and Evans: A Decade of Paintings, catalogue,
Arts Council of Great Britain, 1982

Nicola Lockey, Design and Art, 21 May 1982

Angela Neustatter, Options, December 1982

Mario Amaya, Studio International, April 1984

James Burr, Apollo Magazine, February 1984

Waldemar Januszczak, The Guardian, 3 February 1984

Marina Vaizey, Sunday Times, 12 February 1984

Nigel Pollitt, City Limits, 24 February – 1 March 1984

Michael Shepherd, Sunday Telegraph, 26 February 1984

Bryan Edmondson, Boyd and Evans 1982-1985, catalogue,
Milton Keynes Exhibition Gallery and Drumcroon Art Centre, Wigan, 1985

Mike Evans, Milton Keynes Mirror on Sunday, September 1985

Andy Gibbs, Milton Keynes Gazette, September 1985

David Wright, Arts Review, 25 October 1985

Mel Gooding, Art Monthly, July/August 1986

Mog Johnstone, Artline, Summer 1986

Robert Heller, Boyd and Evans: Paintings 1986-1988, catalogue,
Angela Flowers Gallery, 1988

David Miller, Artscribe, September/October 1988

Patrick Hughes, Bird: Boyd and Evans, catalogue, Flowers Graphics, 1990

Kunstforum, March/April 1990

Guy Burn, Arts Review, 6 April 1990

David Miller, Boyd & Evans catalogue 1991

© COPYRIGHT 1991
BOYD & EVANS,
DAVID MILLER
AND FLOWERS EAST

CATALOGUE DESIGNED BY
THUMB DESIGN PARTNERSHIP
PRINTED BY DOT FOR DOT

PHOTOGRAPHY BY
ADRIAN FLOWERS

ISBN 1 873362 08 0
1250 COPIES